Ss

Bela Davis

Abdo
THE ALPHABET
Kids

abdopublishing.com

Published by Abdo Kids, a division of ABDO, PO Box 398166, Minneapolis, Minnesota 55439.
Copyright © 2017 by Abdo Consulting Group, Inc. International copyrights reserved in all countries.
No part of this book may be reproduced in any form without written permission from the publisher.
Printed in the United States of America, North Mankato, Minnesota.
102016
012017

 THIS BOOK CONTAINS
RECYCLED MATERIALS

Photo Credits: iStock, Shutterstock
Production Contributors: Teddy Borth, Jennie Forsberg, Grace Hansen
Design Contributors: Christina Doffing, Candice Keimig, Dorothy Toth

Publisher's Cataloging in Publication Data
Names: Davis, Bela, author.
Title: Ss / by Bela Davis.
Description: Minneapolis, Minnesota : Abdo Kids, 2017 | Series: The alphabet |
     Includes bibliographical references and index.
Identifiers: LCCN 2016943899 | ISBN 9781680808957 (lib. bdg.) |
     ISBN 9781680796056 (ebook) | ISBN 9781680796728 (Read-to-me ebook)
Subjects: LCSH: English language--Alphabet--Juvenile literature. | Alphabet
     books--Juvenile literature.
Classification: DDC 421/.1--dc23
LC record available at http://lccn.loc.gov/2016943899

Table of Contents

Ss 4

More Ss Words 22

Glossary 23

Index 24

Abdo Kids Code . . . 24

Ss

Sadie act**s s**illy with **S**ara.

Ss

Saul love**s** hi**s** **s**i**s**ter**s**.

6

Ss

Sofia **skips** with a **s**tone.

Ss

Sergio **s**ail**s** in the **s**ea.

Ss

Stella like**s s**occer.

Ss

Seth eat**s** hi**s** **s**upper **s**o fa**s**t!

Ss

Selena i**s** on a **slippery s**lide.

Ss

Sam cool**s** off in the **shade**.

Ss

What is Scott doing?

(singing)

More Ss Words

saddle

starfish

sandwich

stop sign

Glossary

skip
to move by stepping from one foot to the other with a hop.

shade
an area of slight darkness that is made when something blocks light from the sun.

slippery
tending to cause sliding or slipping.

Index

sail 10

sea 10

shade 18

silly 4

sing 20

sister 6

skip 8

slide 16

soccer 12

stone 8

supper 14

abdokids.com

Use this code to log on to abdokids.com and access crafts, games, videos, and more!

Abdo Kids Code:
TSK8957